The Oracle Witch

Divining the Future and Embracing the Unknown

The Oracle Witch: Divining the Future and Embracing the Unknown

Copyright © 2023 Nichole Callaghan

All right reserved. No part of this book may be reproduced by any mechanical, photographic, or electronic process, or in the form of a phonographic recording: nor may it be stored in a retrieval system, transmitted, or otherwise be copied for public or private use- other than for "fair use" as brief quotation embodied in articles and reviews – without prior written permission of the publisher

Please note the information contained within this document is for educational and entertainment purposes only. All effort has been executed to present accurate, up to date, and reliable, complete information. No warranties of any kind are declared or implied.

Readers acknowledge that the author is not engaging in the rendering of legal, financial, medical or professional advice. The content within this book has been derived from various sources. Please consult a licensed professional before attempting any techniques outlined in this book.

Contents

Chapter 1: The Path to Becoming an Oracle Witch 4

Chapter 2: Tools of the Oracle Witch 9

Chapter 3: Grounding and Centering 15

Chapter 4: The Elements and Their Power 20

Chapter 5: The Moon, the Stars, and the Oracle Witch 26

Chapter 6: Enhancing Intuition 31

Chapter 7: Interpreting Signs and Symbols 36

Chapter 8: Creating Sacred Space 41

Chapter 9: The Power of Color in Divination 46

Chapter 10: Animal Guides and Spirit Animals 51

Chapter 11: Working with Spirit Guides and Deities 57

Chapter 12: The Witch's Sabbats and Divination 63

Chapter 13: Scrying – The Ancient Art of Seeing 70

Chapter 14: Tarot Reading for the Oracle Witch 75

Chapter 15: Pendulum Divination 80

Chapter 16: Runes and Ogham – Ancient Scripts for Divination 85

Chapter 17: Embracing the Unknown – The Journey Ahead . 90

Chapter 1: The Path to Becoming an Oracle Witch

What is the path to becoming an Oracle Witch? It's a question often asked, with as many answers as there are stars in the night sky. Each Oracle Witch's journey is as unique as they are, but the foundation remains constant: a deep-rooted connection with nature, an understanding of energy flow, and a reverence for the tools of divination.

At its core, the journey begins with the fundamentals of witchcraft itself. Witchcraft, in its essence, is a craft borne from the earth, nurtured by the elements, and shaped by the energies that bind everything in the universe. It's a practice of manipulating these energies to bring about change, using the inherent power that lies within nature and ourselves.

Witchcraft in its many forms has been practiced for centuries, evolving from ancient pagan rituals to the modern practices we see today. It's rooted in an understanding of the cycles of nature and the universe, the shifting tides of energy that flow through all living things, and the fundamental elements that make up our world.

As an Oracle Witch, you are a diviner, a seer, a conduit between the physical and spiritual realms. You draw on your deep connection with the world around you and use your intuition to interpret the messages that the universe sends your way. This practice of divination, of peering into the future or seeking answers to the present, is as old as humanity itself. The tools may vary, from tarot cards to runes, crystal balls to pendulums, but the goal is the same: to divine the unknown.

In your hands, these tools become more than mere objects. They become extensions of your will, your energy. They are conduits through which you channel the universe's wisdom. But the true tool, the most powerful one, lies within you. It's your intuition, your innate understanding of the world, your connection with the energies that surge around and within you.

The basic elements of nature - Earth, Air, Fire, Water, and Spirit - form the foundation of this craft. Each of these elements carries its unique energy, and as an Oracle Witch, understanding these energies and how to harness them is crucial. The steady, grounding energy of the Earth, the swift, communicating energy of the Air, the transformative, passionate energy of Fire, the emotional, healing energy of Water, and the unifying, transcendent energy of Spirit.

Respect for free will and privacy is a cornerstone of being an Oracle Witch. Divination, at its heart, is a deeply personal and intimate process. It delves into the most profound corners of one's being, revealing truths that may otherwise remain hidden. The Oracle Witch holds the responsibility to respect these truths, to protect the privacy of those who seek their wisdom, and to never use their skills to infringe upon free will. It's an ethic born out of respect for the individual, for the universal balance, and for the craft itself.

Each step on this path, every ritual you perform, every tool you consecrate, every element you invoke, you do so with intention. Intent is a powerful catalyst in witchcraft. It is what directs your energy, what shapes your spells and readings, what infuses your actions with purpose.

In the chapters that follow, we will delve deeper into these concepts. We will explore the art of divination, the use and consecration of various tools, the invocation of the elements, and much more. You will learn to listen to the whispers of the universe, to divine the future, and to tap into your intuition like never before. But remember, the most essential element of this path is you.

You, the Oracle Witch, are a beacon of wisdom in an uncertain world. You are a bridge between the seen and the unseen, a mediator between the past, the present, and the future. You are a weaver of destinies, a reader of the stars, a child of nature, and a conduit of energy. This is your path. Embrace it with an open heart, a clear mind, and an unbroken spirit.

This journey isn't about reaching a destination; it's about the lessons you learn, the wisdom you gain, and the person you become along the way. You are stepping onto a path that has been walked by many before you and will be walked by many after you. It's a path of wisdom, power, responsibility, and mystery. It's the path of the Oracle Witch, divining the future and embracing the unknown. Welcome, and blessed be.

Chapter 2: Tools of the Oracle Witch

The world of the Oracle Witch is steeped in rich traditions and centuries-old practices, harmonizing with the rhythms of nature and celestial movements. However, one of the defining characteristics of an Oracle Witch lies in the use of her tools – implements designed to focus and guide the Witch's intuitive abilities, enhancing her ability to divine the future and embrace the unknown. The tools at an Oracle Witch's disposal are as varied as they are intriguing, ranging from tarot cards, pendulums, scrying mirrors, to crystal balls. Understanding how to choose, cleanse, and consecrate these tools is integral to successful divination.

Tarot Cards

The tarot, with its intricate imagery and deep symbolism, is a classic tool of divination. Tarot decks generally comprise 78 cards, divided into the Major Arcana, representing life's spiritual and karmic lessons, and the Minor Arcana reflecting trials and tribulations of our everyday life.

When choosing a tarot deck, let your intuition guide you. You might be drawn to a deck because of its artwork, its feel in your hands, or a sense of familiarity or connection. Each deck has its unique energy, and the right deck for you is the one that resonates with your spirit.

To cleanse a new tarot deck, you could use incense or sage smoke, sweeping it through the smoke to clear away any negative or stagnant energy. Another method is to leave the deck under the light of the full moon, or bury it in salt or earth.

Consecrating a tarot deck involves imbuing it with your energy. Hold the deck in your hands, infusing it with your intention. Speak your purpose for the deck aloud and ask for clear, helpful guidance during your readings.

Pendulums

A pendulum, often a small weight suspended on a string or chain, is a tool that taps into your subconscious mind. It gives voice to your intuitive feelings and can answer yes or no questions, and sometimes more complex queries.

Choosing a pendulum is an intimate process, as it needs to be tuned to your personal energy. You can use crystals, wood, or metal as pendulums. Like with tarot cards, you might feel a connection or attraction to a particular pendulum.

To cleanse a pendulum, you can use smoke from incense or sage, moonlight, or running water. As pendulums are often made from crystals, check if the material of your pendulum is water-safe before using this method.

When consecrating a pendulum, hold it in your hand and state your intention. Ask the pendulum to work with you to provide clear and truthful answers.

Scrying Mirrors

Scrying mirrors, often called black mirrors, are tools for seeing into the possible future, the past, or the hidden. They serve as a focus point for your intuitive vision.

A scrying mirror can be any reflective black surface. Some people use obsidian or black glass, while others paint a piece of glass or a picture frame. Choose a mirror that feels right to you, one that draws you in when you look into it.

Cleansing a scrying mirror can be done using incense or sage smoke, or by leaving it under the light of the moon. Since this tool is used for vision work, it might also be useful to cleanse it by breathing onto the mirror's surface, using the element of air to clear away any unwanted energies.

To consecrate your scrying mirror, cover the reflective surface and sit with it in meditation. Visualize your energy connecting with the mirror, and when you feel ready, uncover the mirror and gaze into its surface. Ask it to work with you in providing clarity and insight.

Crystal Balls

A crystal ball is perhaps one of the most iconic images when one thinks of divination. This transparent sphere serves as a conduit for the seer's psychic energy, helping to project intuitive images or impressions.

When choosing a crystal ball, take note of how it feels in your hands. Look into the sphere – it should draw you in, making you feel comfortable and connected. Crystal balls can be made of clear quartz, amethyst, smoky quartz, or even glass.

Cleansing a crystal ball can be done with moonlight, or by smudging it with sage or incense. If your sphere is made from a hard mineral like quartz, you could also rinse it in running water.

Consecrating a crystal ball involves sitting with it in meditation, connecting your energy with the crystal. Ask the crystal ball to show you what you need to see and to work with you in your divination.

Understanding your tools is the first step on the path of the Oracle Witch. However, it's important to remember that the power doesn't come from the tools themselves, but from the Witch who wields them. The tools are there to help focus your innate power and intuition. Through practice and experience, you'll deepen your relationship with your tools, becoming an even more proficient Oracle Witch.

Chapter 3: Grounding and Centering

In the practice of witchcraft, and particularly in the path of an Oracle Witch, grounding and centering serve as the bedrock upon which all other activities are built. Without a firm foundation in these skills, your divination can become unclear, your rituals unfocused, and your connection to the natural world weakened. But with consistent practice, grounding and centering can anchor you in your spiritual path, enhance your intuition, and provide a reservoir of calm and clarity to draw upon when you engage in your craft.

Grounding is the practice of connecting with the Earth and the physical world, drawing energy from them, and returning excess energy to them. It helps to stabilize your energy, align your spiritual self with your physical surroundings, and replenish your inner reservoir of energy. Centering, on the other hand, is the process of bringing your consciousness to a calm and focused state, centered within your own being. Together, these two practices are essential to balancing your energies and ensuring you are in the right state of mind and spirit for any magical work.

Grounding

Before we delve into practical exercises, let's explore the concept of grounding further. Grounding allows us to tap into the energy of the Earth, to align ourselves with the steady, solid, life-giving energy that infuses every rock, tree, and blade of grass. It offers us a way to both draw strength and to discharge surplus energy safely, providing equilibrium.

There are many ways to ground oneself, but one of the most common and effective methods is the

Tree of Life Meditation. This visualization exercise allows us to establish a deep connection with the Earth and attune our energies to its rhythm.

Tree of Life Meditation

Sit or stand comfortably, ensuring your back is straight. If you're sitting, make sure your feet are flat on the floor. Close your eyes and take a deep breath in, then let it out slowly. Repeat this a few times until you feel yourself begin to relax.

Imagine that you are a tree. Visualize roots growing from your feet, pushing through the floor and down into the Earth. Feel them penetrate the soil, pushing through layers of rock, clay, and sand until they reach the very heart of the Earth.

With every breath in, draw up the Earth's energy along these roots, letting it flow into you, filling you from your feet upward. With every breath out, let any tension, negativity, or surplus energy flow down these roots and into the Earth.

Maintain this visualization for a few minutes. When you are ready, slowly retract your roots, pulling them back into your body. Feel the sensation of your feet on the floor once more, anchoring you in the physical world.

Centering

Just as grounding connects us with the Earth, centering connects us with ourselves. The purpose of centering is to draw our awareness inward, to a place of calm and balance. We can think of this place as our spiritual center of gravity – a point within us that is still, serene, and imbued with our purest self.

One powerful way of centering is the Sphere of Light Meditation, which helps to gather scattered energies and thoughts, focusing them into a concentrated sphere of consciousness.

Sphere of Light Meditation

Sit comfortably with your feet flat on the floor. Close your eyes and take several deep, calming breaths.

Imagine a sphere of light in the center of your being, perhaps in your heart or your solar plexus. This light represents your energy, your consciousness, your spirit.

With each breath in, see the sphere become brighter. With each breath out, imagine the light expanding a little, growing until it fills your whole body.

As the light fills you, let it gather any scattered thoughts, any stray emotions or energies, pulling them in and incorporating them into the sphere.

When you are ready, imagine the sphere contracting again, pulling back to its original size, but brighter and stronger for having gathered your scattered energies. Sit with this feeling for a moment, enjoying the sense of centered calm.

Grounding and centering are not one-time exercises, but practices to be incorporated into your daily life. They are the key to maintaining balance and focus, crucial for the work of an Oracle Witch. These techniques root us in the present moment, connect us to the world around us, and align our energies, preparing us for the magical work ahead.

In the following chapters, we will explore divination and other facets of witchcraft, all of which will be enhanced by the practices of grounding and centering. Remember, the journey of the Oracle Witch is not merely about predicting the future; it's about fully engaging with the present moment, connected to both the physical world and your own inner self. By mastering grounding and centering, you are taking important steps on this path.

Chapter 4: The Elements and Their Power

The foundation of any potent witchcraft practice lies in understanding and harnessing the forces of the natural world. At the heart of these forces are the four classical elements: Earth, Air, Fire, and Water. These elements are not merely physical entities, but powerful symbols representing different states of energy, and aspects of life.

Earth – The Element of Stability and Grounding

The element of Earth represents stability, grounding, fertility, materiality, and potential. It is associated with the physical body, nature, and the nurturing aspect of the universe. Its qualities are solidity, permanence, endurance, and practicality. The Earth is receptive, absorbing energy and nutrients, transforming them into nourishment and life.

In the realm of divination, the Earth element helps us connect with our senses and the physical world around us. Its grounding influence can help stabilize turbulent emotions and clarify muddled thoughts. Rituals and spells associated with the Earth element often involve materials like stones, crystals, plants, and soil.

Earth Element Ritual

To harness the grounding energy of the Earth, perform this ritual. You will need a small stone or crystal, preferably one you have found in nature. Hold the stone in your hands, close your eyes, and visualize energy flowing from your body into the stone. Picture your worries, fears, and uncertainties seeping out of you and into the rock. When you open your eyes, bury the stone in the ground, symbolically letting go of those burdens.

Air – The Element of Intellect and Communication

Air is the element of intellect, creativity, and communication. It represents thoughts, ideas, dreams, wishes, and the powers of the mind. Air is associated with motion, flexibility, and the breath of life. In divination, the Air element can guide us in seeking wisdom and clarity.

Air Element Ritual

To connect with the Air element, find a place where you can feel the wind, such as a hilltop or open field. Stand with your arms open wide, facing into the wind. Close your eyes and take a deep breath, filling your lungs with air. As you exhale, visualize the wind carrying away your thoughts, leaving your mind clear and open.

Fire – The Element of Transformation and Passion

Fire embodies transformation, passion, energy, motivation, willpower, and creativity. It is a powerful force that can both create and destroy. In divination, Fire can spark insight, ignite passion, and fuel determination.

Fire Element Ritual

This Fire ritual is best performed with a candle. Light the candle and focus on the flame. Visualize what you desire — whether it's a change in your life, the strength to overcome a challenge, or a boost of creativity. Imagine the flame growing brighter with your desire, the fire's energy feeding your intention. As the candle burns, it releases your intention into the universe.

Water – The Element of Emotion and Intuition

Water, the element of emotion, intuition, compassion, and the subconscious, is fluid, adaptable, and cleansing. It can be tranquil or tumultuous, gentle or powerful. In divination, the Water element aids in tapping into our intuition, unearthing deep emotions, and healing emotional wounds.

Water Element Ritual

A simple way to connect with the Water element is through a cleansing bath. Fill a tub with warm water and add sea salt, which has purifying properties. As you submerge yourself in the water, imagine it washing away negativity, stress, and emotional pain. When you drain the bath, visualize these things going down the drain, leaving you cleansed and revitalized.

Incorporating the Elements into Divination

Incorporating the elements into your divination practice can greatly enhance your readings. Each element can be invoked depending on what you seek. If you're looking for stability and practicality in your decision-making, call upon Earth. If you're seeking clear communication and intellectual growth, invoke Air. If you want to ignite your passion or instigate change, call upon Fire. And if you're seeking emotional healing or intuitive insight, invoke Water.

You can invoke these elements by placing representative items on your divination altar, reciting element-focused incantations, or performing the aforementioned rituals before divination. For example, a crystal or plant could represent Earth, incense or a feather could represent Air, a candle or ash could represent Fire, and a bowl of water or a seashell could represent Water.

By incorporating these elements into your divination practice, you deepen your connection with nature and the universe, and, in turn, strengthen your readings and your own intuition.

Remember that it is through the combination of these elements that life as we know it exists – and it is through understanding them that we can divine more profound truths about our own existence.

Chapter 5: The Moon, the Stars, and the Oracle Witch

The cosmos holds a profound influence on our lives. As an Oracle Witch, you not only acknowledge this influence but actively invite it into your divination practices. When we learn to read the language of the celestial bodies, our understanding of the world around us and our place within it deepens significantly.

One of the most influential celestial bodies in witchcraft and divination is the Moon. This glowing orb has been a source of wonder and inspiration for humans since the dawn of time. The Moon's phases – new, waxing, full, and waning – have been observed and honored in many cultures and spiritual practices, including witchcraft.

Understanding the Lunar Cycle

The lunar cycle is approximately 28 days long, mirroring many natural rhythms on Earth. Each phase of the Moon holds unique energy that can be harnessed in your divination practices:

The New Moon: Symbolizes new beginnings and fresh starts. It's a time to set intentions and start new projects.

Waxing Moon: As the moon grows larger in the sky, it represents growth, manifestation, and creativity. This is an ideal time to take action toward the intentions set during the New Moon.

Full Moon: This phase represents completion, fruition, and enlightenment. It's a powerful time for divination, as intuitive energies are at their peak.

Waning Moon: As the moon decreases in size, it signifies release, letting go, and introspection. It's an excellent time to reflect on what no longer serves you and to release it.

Ritual for Harnessing Lunar Energy

The Moon's energy can be harnessed through various rituals and can significantly enhance your divination practices. Here is a simple ritual to connect with the lunar cycle:

Begin by setting up a sacred space where you won't be disturbed. Light a white or silver candle to represent the Moon's energy. Sit comfortably and take a few moments to ground and center yourself. Hold a moonstone or clear quartz in your hands (both are linked with lunar energy) and gaze at the Moon (if visible) or visualize it in your mind's eye.

Speak aloud or silently express your intention to connect with the Moon's energy. For example, during a Full Moon, you might ask for clarity and insight in your divination practices. During the Waning Moon, you might seek assistance in releasing doubt or fear about your intuitive abilities.

Spend a few moments in silent meditation, visualizing the Moon's light washing over you, imbuing you with its energy. Thank the Moon for its guidance and gently extinguish the candle.

Astrological Influences

Beyond the Moon, the other celestial bodies in our solar system – the Sun and the planets – and the twelve constellations of the zodiac also influence us. Each planet governs certain aspects of life, and its position in a specific zodiac sign at a given time can affect our behaviors, emotions, and situations.

Astrology can be an invaluable tool for the Oracle Witch, offering insight into how cosmic forces might be influencing a situation or person at a given time. The planets' energy can be harnessed to enhance your divination practices. For example, if you're conducting a tarot reading to gain insight into a relationship during Venus retrograde, you might take into account that this is a time when past relationships can resurface or current relationships may be tested.

Planetary Hours and Days

Each day of the week is associated with a particular planet and its corresponding energy. These connections can be used to enhance your divination practices. For example, conducting divination on a Monday – associated with the Moon – can be particularly potent for intuitive and psychic work.

Similarly, each hour of the day holds a planetary association, rotating through the seven traditional 'planetary' bodies – the Sun, the Moon, Mars, Mercury, Jupiter, Venus, and Saturn. If you choose to perform a divination ritual during a specific planetary hour, it can bring the energy of that planet to your work.

By understanding and harnessing the power of celestial bodies, you'll infuse your divination practices with the ancient wisdom of the cosmos. The Moon, the stars, and the planets offer us their guidance and insights – as an Oracle Witch, all you need to do is to look up and listen.

Chapter 6: Enhancing Intuition

An Oracle Witch depends upon intuition as much as any tool in their arsenal. The intuitive mind is like a compass, guiding us toward truth and wisdom. The ability to tune into this intuition, to listen and to understand its language, is a skill that can be honed and refined. This chapter delves into ways to enhance intuition, offering exercises to develop psychic abilities, meditation techniques, and rituals to open the third eye chakra.

Intuition, often termed as the sixth sense, transcends the realm of the five conventional senses. It's an instinctive awareness providing insight about our surroundings and the course of events. As Oracle Witches, we harness intuition to perceive and interpret the mystical signs and symbols that ordinary eyes might overlook.

The first step to enhancing intuition is recognizing its existence and understanding its importance. For an Oracle Witch, intuition can act as a guiding light. But how can we strengthen this light? How can we make it shine brighter and more reliably?

Awareness and Mindfulness

Developing awareness is the starting point. We're often so immersed in our everyday hustle that we tend to ignore the subtle whispers of intuition. Begin by paying attention to your feelings, thoughts, and bodily sensations throughout the day. This increased awareness can provide a fertile ground for intuition to grow.

Practice mindfulness. This is about being fully present in each moment, being aware of where you are, what you're doing, and how you're feeling. Mindfulness brings you into closer alignment with your intuition, by reducing the noise of distracting thoughts.

Meditation

Meditation serves as a powerful tool to enhance intuition. By quieting the mind, we allow the softer voice of intuition to emerge.

Try a simple mindfulness meditation. Begin by sitting comfortably in a quiet space. Close your eyes and take slow, deep breaths. Allow your attention to rest on the sensation of your breath entering and leaving your body. Whenever your mind wanders, gently bring it back to the breath. Practicing this meditation regularly can create a serene mental space for your intuition to grow stronger.

Dream Work

Our intuition often speaks to us through our dreams. Begin a dream journal and make a habit of recording your dreams upon waking. Pay attention to patterns, symbols, or messages in your dreams. They can provide significant insight into your intuitive mind.

Ritual for Opening the Third Eye Chakra

The Third Eye Chakra, also known as Anja, is often associated with intuition, foresight, and spiritual enlightenment. By opening and balancing this chakra, we can enhance our intuitive abilities. Here is a ritual for doing just that:

Setting the Stage: Begin by preparing a quiet and peaceful environment. Dim the lights, light a purple or indigo candle (representative of the Third Eye Chakra's color), and if you wish, play some soft, ambient music.

The Cleansing Breath: Sit comfortably with your spine straight. Close your eyes and take deep, cleansing breaths. With each exhale, visualize any negativity or blockages leaving your body.

Third Eye Visualization: Visualize an indigo orb of light in the middle of your forehead, the location of your Third Eye Chakra. See this orb growing brighter and larger with each breath.

The Affirmation: As you maintain this visualization, silently repeat the following affirmation: "I am open to the wisdom within. I trust my intuition and follow its guidance."

Closing the Ritual: When you feel ready, gently bring your attention back to your physical surroundings. Snuff out the candle to symbolically close the ritual.

It's essential to remember that developing intuition is a process. With practice and patience, your intuitive abilities will grow. As an Oracle Witch, enhanced intuition will empower your divination practices, enrich your personal growth, and help you navigate the world with heightened awareness and insight.

As you progress on this path, embrace the journey. Remember, intuition is not about having all the answers, but rather knowing that you can find them. By nurturing your intuition, you're nurturing an intimate relationship with your inner Oracle Witch, ready to divine the future and embrace the unknown.

Chapter 7: Interpreting Signs and Symbols

Interpreting signs and symbols, as we delve deeper into the realm of divination, is a critical step towards understanding the messages and guidance being channeled from the universe. This chapter will journey through the ancient art of interpreting symbols in tarot cards and runes, two common tools of divination for an Oracle Witch. We will explore their mysterious languages and how they can help us unveil the concealed and the unknown.

Tarot Symbolism

One of the richest and most versatile divination tools is the tarot deck. Comprising 78 cards divided into the Major and Minor Arcana, each card in a tarot deck is packed with a variety of symbols that can interpret complex life situations and the human psyche.

Major Arcana Symbolism

The Major Arcana, often referred to as the "Soul's Journey," consists of 22 cards starting from The Fool (0 or 22) to The World (21). Each card represents a stage in this journey, encompassing key spiritual lessons and life experiences.

For instance, The Fool symbolizes beginnings, spontaneity, and faith in the universe. It's often depicted as a young man stepping off a cliff with a small bag (symbolizing untapped potential) and a white rose (purity and innocence) in his hands. A small dog accompanies him, embodying loyalty and protection.

However, it's important to note that symbols in tarot are not standalone; their meanings can change depending on the other cards in the spread. For example, if The Fool shows up with The Tower (a symbol of sudden upheaval), it might suggest a leap of faith that leads to unexpected chaos.

Minor Arcana Symbolism

The Minor Arcana, divided into four suits (Cups, Wands, Swords, and Pentacles), represents daily life occurrences and our reactions to them. Each suit is associated with an element and symbolizes different aspects of human experience.

Cups, tied to the water element, embody emotions and relationships. Swords, associated with air, represent thoughts, intellect, and conflict. Wands, connected to fire, symbolize creativity, passion, and action. Lastly, Pentacles, linked with earth, signify material aspects, including work and finances.

Runic Symbolism

Runes, derived from ancient alphabets, are another powerful tool for divination. Each rune, with its distinctive symbol, carries complex meanings and associations, ranging from concepts, events, to natural forces.

For example, the rune Fehu, resembling a domestic cattle, symbolizes wealth and abundance. However, like tarot symbols, this doesn't merely denote material prosperity. It could also refer to spiritual wealth and personal growth. Similarly, the rune Thurisaz, symbolizing a thorn or a giant, speaks of reactive forces, conflict, and hardship.

Remember that each rune has both a conventional meaning and a "reversed" or "merkstave" meaning. This duality reflects the multifaceted nature of life experiences, urging us to examine situations from different angles.

Interpreting Patterns

When divining, whether through tarot or runes, it's not just individual signs and symbols that matter; the patterns they form and their interactions are equally significant.

In a tarot spread, if multiple cards from the same suit appear, they emphasize a particular area of life. For instance, numerous Cups might suggest the issue revolves around relationships or emotions. Similarly, in a runic reading, if you see several runes connected to change and transformation, like Hagalaz (hail) or Jera (year or harvest), you might be undergoing a significant life transition.

Spatial relationships between the cards or runes also matter. In tarot, a card following another can suggest a causal relationship, while in runes, two runes touching each other can mean their energies are blending or clashing.

Interpreting signs, symbols, and patterns in divination is like learning a new language - one that communicates through images and associations rather than words. It's a language of the subconscious, of the universe, whispered to us through the cards and runes.

It takes time and practice to understand this symbolic language. Each reading you perform will improve your understanding and interpretation of these symbols, making you more fluent. As with any language, immersion and regular practice are the keys to proficiency. Don't rush the process, allow yourself to grow naturally into your role as an Oracle Witch.

In the next chapters, we will continue to deepen our understanding of these symbols and how they interact within sacred spaces and rituals. The journey is endless and profound, but every step is a revelation, a step closer to wisdom and self-discovery.

Chapter 8: Creating Sacred Space

Creating a sacred space is a significant practice for an Oracle Witch. It is the platform upon which all magic is conducted. In witchcraft, we create this space, or circle, not just for protection, but to distinguish between our mundane lives and our spiritual practice. The act of creating a sacred space helps to shift our consciousness, preparing our minds and spirits for the work ahead. In this chapter, we'll explore the process of setting up an altar, casting a circle, and creating wards for protection.

Setting Up an Altar

The altar is the heart of your sacred space, the focal point where you direct your energies and perform your work. It can be as simple or as elaborate as you want it to be, and it should reflect your personal beliefs and the intention behind your practices.

To start, choose a location for your altar. This could be a small table, a shelf, or even a space on the floor—any place that can hold your sacred items. Many witches prefer to place their altars facing North, the direction associated with the element of Earth and the qualities of grounding and stability. However, you may choose to align your altar with the direction that resonates most with your current intention.

Next, cleanse the space. You can do this with a simple ritual using your preferred method—smudging with sage or palo santo, asperging with saltwater, or energetically sweeping the area with your hands or a ritual broom.

Once the space is cleansed, you can start placing your tools and symbols. Many witches like to represent the four elements—Earth, Air, Fire, and Water—on their altars. A dish of salt or soil, a feather or incense, a candle or wand, and a chalice or bowl of water are common representations, respectively. Central to your altar could be your Book of Shadows, Oracle or Tarot cards, or any other divination tool you regularly use.

Casting a Circle

With your altar set up, you're ready to cast your circle. This ritual action serves to demarcate your sacred space, keeping out any unwanted energies and keeping in your own energy until your work is complete. It also serves to focus your mind and mark the transition from the mundane to the sacred.

Stand at your altar and close your eyes, grounding yourself by imagining roots growing from your feet into the earth. Take your ritual blade or wand (or your index finger, if you prefer), and starting from the North, move deosil (clockwise) around your space, visualizing a circle of light emanating from your tool and encompassing your area.

As you cast the circle, you may wish to call upon the elements, the guardians of the watchtowers, or any other entities or deities you work with. An example invocation might be:

"I cast this circle of light to protect me in my work. I call upon the powers of Earth, Air, Fire, and Water to guard this space and guide my intentions. As I will, so mote it be."

Once your circle is cast, you're ready to conduct your ritual or divination work within it.

Creating Wards

Wards are energetic barriers you place around your home, your ritual space, or even yourself for protection. Think of them as spiritual security systems. Wards can be created in many ways, but the most common is by using symbols or sigils imbued with your intention.

To create a ward, first decide on the symbol you want to use. This could be a traditional sigil, a rune, or even a picture that represents protection to you. Once you've chosen your symbol, spend some time meditating on it and charging it with your protective intent.

Next, using a consecrated tool, draw or etch your symbol at the points you wish to protect. If you're warding your home, this might be on the doors and windows. If you're warding your ritual space, it could be on the boundaries of the area, or even on the tools you use within the space.

As you place each ward, visualize it glowing with protective energy, forming an impenetrable barrier against any unwanted or harmful forces. You might also choose to say a few words as you place each ward, such as:

"By this symbol, I ward this space. Only love and light may enter, all else is turned away. As I will, so mote it be."

Remember, the power of the ward comes not from the symbol itself, but from the intent behind it.

Creating a sacred space is a deeply personal act and a fundamental part of the Oracle Witch's practice. Take your time with it, make it your own, and know that you are creating a place where you can connect with the divine, tap into your intuition, and perform your magical work.

Chapter 9: The Power of Color in Divination

Colors speak a language of their own. They are carriers of energy, emotion, and information, and in the realm of the Oracle Witch, they hold a special significance. Each color resonates with a unique frequency that aligns with specific aspects of our life, emotions, spiritual states, and psychological conditions. By understanding and applying the power of colors, you can bring greater depth, clarity, and insight to your divination practices.

Red, the color of fire, represents passion, energy, strength, and courage. It is the color of life-blood, of vitality, and physical presence. In divination, red can denote immediate action, strong emotions, or matters of survival and physical health.

Orange, the color of the rising or setting sun, symbolizes creativity, joy, and social connections. It represents the sacral chakra, the energetic center related to pleasure, desire, and creativity. In a divination reading, orange might point towards issues or opportunities related to relationships, enjoyment, or artistic pursuits.

Yellow, akin to a high-noon sun, speaks to intellect, personal power, and confidence. This bright color is linked to the solar plexus chakra, the center of personal power and self-esteem. Yellow in a reading could suggest intellectual pursuits, the need for clear thinking, or an increase in personal power or confidence.

Green resonates with the heart chakra and is deeply tied to love, compassion, and healing. The color of nature, green symbolizes growth and abundance. In divination, green might indicate growth, healing, prosperity, or matters of the heart.

Blue, like the expansive sky or deep sea, is the color of communication, truth, and intuition. Associated with the throat chakra, blue in divination might suggest issues or opportunities related to communication, speaking one's truth, or spiritual insight.

Indigo, a deeper blue, links to the third eye chakra and stands for intuition, perception, and wisdom. In divination, indigo may hint at a need for deeper insight, developing intuition, or understanding the bigger picture.

Purple, or violet, is the color of the crown chakra, symbolizing spirituality, connection to the divine, and enlightenment. It represents the ethereal, the magical, and the transcendent. In divination, purple may suggest spiritual growth, the need for reflection, or the presence of magic and transformation.

White is the color of purity, cleansing, and protection. In divination, white can denote new beginnings, spiritual protection, or the need for cleansing and purification.

Black, often misunderstood, is the color of the unknown, the subconscious, and protection. It represents mystery, the void from which all creation springs. In divination, black can point to hidden things, unconscious patterns, or the need for protection.

Let's explore a color meditation and ritual that can be incorporated into your divination practice.

Color Meditation

Begin by choosing a color you feel drawn to or one you want to understand better. Sit comfortably in a quiet place, close your eyes, and visualize a ball of light in the chosen color. Imagine this colored light growing and filling the room, engulfing you in its glow.

Feel its energy, its vibration, and let it resonate within you. Ask the color to show you its energy, its messages. Be open to emotions, images, or thoughts that may arise. They are the color speaking to you, revealing its secrets. When you feel complete, let the color slowly fade, leaving its wisdom within you.

Color Ritual

For this ritual, gather candles in various colors, a white cloth, and your divination tool of choice.

Spread the white cloth on your sacred space or altar. Arrange your candles on the cloth, creating a circle. Light the candles, starting with the one that aligns with your current question or situation. If you are unsure, light a white candle.

As the candle burns, focus on its color, the flame, and what they represent. Hold your divination tool in your hands and ask your question. Let the color's energy guide your insights as you use your divination tool.

Colors, with their vibrational energy, are an invaluable resource in your journey as an Oracle Witch. By incorporating their energy into your divination practices, you enhance your ability to connect with the universal energies and interpret the wisdom they offer.

Remember, the language of colors is nuanced, and as you continue your practice, you will deepen your understanding and personal connection to the myriad shades and tints. Trust your intuition, for color, like every aspect of divination, is a deeply personal and subjective realm. Embrace the full spectrum, for every color has its place in the great tapestry of divination and the universe.

Chapter 10: Animal Guides and Spirit Animals

The natural world is rich with wisdom and energy. As Oracle Witches, we often tap into the incredible power that flows through every tree, river, mountain, and creature. This chapter explores one of the most enchanting aspects of this relationship with nature – animal guides and spirit animals.

Understanding Animal Guides and Spirit Animals

Animal guides, also known as power animals or spirit animals, are spiritual entities that offer guidance, protection, and companionship to those who seek it. These creatures often embody characteristics or abilities we need to cultivate in ourselves. They offer insight into our subconscious minds, teaching us about our strengths, vulnerabilities, and paths for growth.

Every culture has its interpretations and traditions involving animal spirits. Native American cultures, for example, have a deep-seated belief in animal totems, viewing them as protectors, ancestors, or guides. Similarly, Celtic druids revered the power and wisdom of animals, and their folklore is rich with animal symbolism.

It's important to note that everyone can have more than one animal guide. Different animal spirits may come to you throughout your life, each one appearing at a time when its specific energies, lessons, or support are needed.

Connecting With Your Spirit Animal

Identifying and connecting with your spirit animal is a deeply personal and transformative experience. Here are some steps to help you in this journey:

Intention and Meditation: As with any spiritual work, the first step is to set a clear intention. What are you seeking? Why do you want to connect with your spirit animal? Once your intention is clear, find a quiet space where you can meditate without interruption.

Enter a meditative state by focusing on your breath or visualizing a peaceful scene. Call upon your guides and ask that your spirit animal make itself known to you. Allow images, feelings, or thoughts to flow freely. Don't force anything; just open yourself up to receive.

Dream Work: Our dreams are a direct line to our subconscious and a channel for spiritual communication. Before sleeping, ask your spirit animal to reveal itself in your dream. Keep a dream journal nearby to record any significant symbols, emotions, or events.

Observation: Pay attention to the animals that cross your path frequently, whether physically or symbolically. Do you keep seeing images of a specific animal? Do you encounter a particular animal often? These could be signs.

Interpreting Messages from Animal Guides

Each animal guide carries a unique set of symbolism and messages, and their presence in your life can shed light on various aspects of your journey. For instance, a hawk might be guiding you to take a broader perspective, while a wolf may emphasize the importance of community and loyalty.

One of the best ways to interpret these messages is through meditation and journaling. After a meditation session where an animal guide appears, take the time to write about the experience. Note your initial feelings about the animal, the setting of your encounter, and any specific actions it took.

Next, consider the characteristics and behaviors of this animal. What is it known for in the natural world? How does its behavior resonate with your current circumstances or questions? A good reference book on animal symbolism can provide insights, but remember to trust your intuition. Your personal connection to the animal will often reveal the most meaningful interpretation.

Ritual to Call Upon Animal Energy

You can also perform a ritual to call upon your animal guide's energy, particularly when you need their specific strength or wisdom. Here's a simple ritual to help you:

Prepare your sacred space as you normally would, making sure to include representations of the four elements. Also, include an item symbolizing your animal guide, like a picture or a figurine.

Cast your circle and call upon the elements and any deities or spirit guides you work with. State your intention clearly, mentioning the animal guide you wish to connect with.

Enter a meditative state, visualizing your animal guide. Invite it into your circle. Speak from your heart, expressing why you seek its energy.

Spend some time in quiet meditation, allowing your animal guide to communicate with you. It may offer guidance, reassurance, or simply its presence.

Once you feel the ritual is complete, thank your animal guide for its presence and wisdom. Close the circle, grounding yourself before leaving your sacred space.

Remember, your relationship with your animal guides is like any other relationship: it requires respect, patience, and time. Connect regularly with them, and remain open to the wisdom they have to offer. The animal kingdom is rich with diverse energies and lessons. As you deepen your understanding and connections, you'll find they are a profound source of guidance, supporting your journey as an Oracle Witch.

Chapter 11: Working with Spirit Guides and Deities

In the vast and intricate world of divination, one facet shines exceptionally brightly: the realm of spirit guides and deities. These luminous entities serve as protectors, teachers, and sources of divine wisdom. As an Oracle Witch, learning to communicate with them can deepen your spiritual practice and enhance your ability to divine the future. This chapter will guide you through this mystical realm, providing rituals for invoking deities and meditations to connect with spirit guides.

First, let's delve into understanding these two distinct entities.

Spirit Guides

Spirit guides are non-physical entities that we are believed to choose before we incarnate into our physical lives. These guides are entrusted with the task of helping us navigate the spiritual and physical worlds, guiding us through challenges, and helping us fulfill our life's purpose. Spirit guides can take many forms: they may be ancestral spirits, spirits of the land, animal spirits, angels, ascended masters, or enlightened beings who have never incarnated on Earth.

Deities

Deities are divine beings that embody universal principles or concepts. They are revered across cultures and throughout history. As an Oracle Witch, you may feel called to connect with a particular deity due to your cultural heritage, personal interests, or specific areas of your craft. Deities can embody a variety of aspects such as love, war, wisdom, nature, and the cycle of life and death. It is crucial to approach them with the utmost respect and reverence.

Connecting with Your Spirit Guide: A Meditation

The first step towards working with spirit guides is making a connection. You might have one or more guides, each assisting with different aspects of your life. The following meditation will help you initiate a dialogue with them.

Find a quiet and comfortable space where you can meditate without interruption. Set the atmosphere by lighting some incense or a candle if you wish. Sit comfortably and take a few deep breaths to center yourself.

Imagine a white, radiant light descending from above, enveloping you in its warmth and protection. This light represents the divine energy that connects all beings. Feel your awareness shift from the physical realm to the spiritual as you sit within this light.

Now, set the intention to meet your spirit guide. You might say something like, "I open myself to connect with my spirit guide who is here for my highest good." Keep your mind open, calm, and receptive.

You may see, feel, or hear your guide, or you may just know that they are there. Don't rush the process. The connection with spirit guides often begins subtly and deepens over time. Ask them any questions you have, listen for their guidance, and express your gratitude for their help.

When you are ready, imagine the divine light gently ascending, bringing your consciousness back to the physical realm. Feel your presence in your body and in the room around you.

Invoking Deities: A Ritual

The ritual for invoking deities is a deeply personal one and it can vary widely depending on your tradition and the deity you're working with. However, a basic structure often includes an offering, invocation, and gratitude.

Begin by preparing your sacred space. This could be an altar dedicated to the deity or a clean, quiet place where you won't be disturbed. Make sure to have an image or symbol of the deity, along with offerings such as food, drink, incense, or flowers.

Stand or sit before your space, ground yourself, and clear your mind. Call upon the deity with respect and sincerity. You may want to use a traditional invocation, or you can create your own. Speak from your heart. Here's an example:

"I call upon you, [Deity's name], with respect and reverence. I seek your wisdom and guidance. Please join me here and now in this sacred space."

Now, present your offerings to the deity. As you do, express your gratitude and state your purpose for seeking their presence. You might ask for guidance, assistance in your craft, or simply seek to honor them.

Spend some time in the deity's presence. Be open to any signs, messages, or feelings you might receive.

To close the ritual, express your gratitude to the deity. You might say:

"Thank you, [Deity's name], for your presence, your guidance, and your wisdom. I honor you and appreciate your aid. Farewell for now, and may we meet again in love and respect."

Remember, the relationship with a deity or spirit guide is like any other—it requires time, patience, respect, and effort to develop. Regularly connect with them through meditation, offerings, and invocation. With time, you'll find your connection deepening and your divination skills improving as you open yourself up to their guidance.

In the next chapter, we will explore how the timing of our rituals and divination can be enhanced by aligning with the cycles of nature, through the eight sabbats of the Wheel of the Year.

Chapter 12: The Witch's Sabbats and Divination

The wheel of the year, marked by the eight sabbats, is a continuous cycle of birth, death, and rebirth, a profound representation of the cyclical nature of life itself. Each sabbat carries a distinctive energy, resonating with specific aspects of our existence, and consequently, with our divination practices.

The sabbats, often celebrated with rituals, feasts, and community gatherings, offer fertile ground to deepen our understanding of divination. They provide ideal moments to connect with the energies of nature and the universe, to seek guidance for the future, and to reflect on the past.

Starting with Samhain and moving deosil (clockwise) around the wheel, let's explore each sabbat, its significance, and its correlation with divination.

Samhain (October 31)

Often considered the witch's new year, Samhain is a time when the veil between our world and the spirit world is at its thinnest. This makes it an ideal time for divination, as communicating with ancestors, spirit guides, and the departed becomes more accessible.

Ritual: Set up your altar with photographs of departed loved ones, candles, and a dish of pomegranate seeds as an offering. Light the candles and focus your mind. Invite the spirits to guide you in your divination. Using tarot or other divination tools, ask about your spiritual growth and insights you should carry into the new year.

Meditation: Sit comfortably in your sacred space and focus on your breath. Visualize the energy of your ancestors merging with your own, opening channels of wisdom and guidance.

Yule (December 21 or 22)

Also known as the Winter Solstice, Yule marks the shortest day of the year. It signifies rebirth and new beginnings, making it a great time for divination related to personal growth and new projects.

Ritual: Create a Yule log with greenery and candles. As you light each candle, ask a question about what the new solar year will bring. Use a pendulum or your intuition to interpret the flame's behavior.

Meditation: Sit in a dimly lit room with a single candle. As you meditate, focus on the flame, drawing in its light and warmth. Imagine this light spreading throughout your body, kindling your own inner light.

Imbolc (February 2)

Imbolc, also known as Candlemas, is a time of purification and clearing away the old to make way for new growth. It is ideal for divinations related to healing, personal cleansing, and home.

Ritual: Light a white candle and cleanse your divination tools in its flame (carefully and without causing damage). Ask for insights about what needs to be healed or cleared away.

Meditation: Visualize a brilliant white light surrounding you, permeating you, purifying your energy. Feel any negativity or blockages dissolving away.

Ostara (March 21 or 22)

Ostara, or the Spring Equinox, is a time of balance and new beginnings. Divination at this time often focuses on personal growth, balance, and creativity.

Ritual: Plant seeds in a pot, each one representing a goal or aspiration. As they grow, so too will your intentions manifest. Use a divination tool to seek guidance on how best to nurture your plans.

Meditation: Meditate on a blossoming flower, visualizing yourself unfolding and growing in the same way, opening up to new possibilities.

Beltane (May 1)

Beltane is a celebration of fertility, abundance, and the burgeoning life of spring. It's a perfect time for divination around love, passion, prosperity, and personal growth.

Ritual: Light a Beltane fire (or a candle if a fire isn't practical). Write questions about your personal or financial growth on bay leaves and toss them into the fire. The manner in which they burn will provide your answers.

Meditation: Envision a growing flame within you, sparking creativity, passion, and abundance. Feel its warmth radiating throughout your being.

Litha (June 21 or 22)

Litha, the Summer Solstice, is a time of power and magic, marking the sun at its zenith. It is an excellent time for divinations regarding power, strength, and transformation.

Ritual: At noon, when the sun is at its highest, perform a sun-mirror ritual. Reflect the sunlight onto a chosen surface and use it as a scrying mirror to gain insights into your personal power and how you can harness it.

Meditation: Sit under the sun (but not to the point of discomfort). Absorb its energy and visualize it amplifying your personal power, resilience, and inner radiance.

Lammas (August 1)

Also known as Lughnasadh, Lammas celebrates the first harvest. It's a time to give thanks and to start reaping what we've sown, both literally and metaphorically. It's suitable for divination around gratitude, harvesting intentions, and planning for the future.

Ritual: Bake a loaf of bread, imbuing it with your intentions. As it bakes, perform a tarot or rune reading to gain insights into the "harvest" that awaits you in the coming months.

Meditation: Meditate on the feeling of gratitude. Envision each thing you are thankful for as a golden grain in a vast field, contributing to your personal abundance.

Mabon (September 21 or 22)

Mabon, or the Autumn Equinox, marks the second harvest. It's a time of balance, introspection, and preparation for the darker months. It's ideal for divination related to self-reflection, balance, and spiritual understanding.

Ritual: Balance a stone on its edge to symbolize the equinox's balance. Perform a divination asking for guidance on how to maintain balance in your life as the wheel turns toward darkness.

Meditation: Meditate on a falling leaf, observing its descent – the perfect balance of gravity and air. As you do so, contemplate the balances within your life.

Embracing these sabbats and aligning your divination practices with their energies can create a more profound, meaningful connection with the natural and spiritual world. As an Oracle Witch, you learn to tap into the flow of the seasons, resonating with the universe's rhythms, your insights deepening with each turn of the wheel.

Chapter 13: Scrying - The Ancient Art of Seeing

The ability to divine the future has been a sought-after skill for millennia. Of the many methods practiced, scrying stands out as one of the most captivating. This practice, which dates back to ancient times, encompasses the art of looking into a suitable medium to detect significant messages or visions.

What is Scrying?

Scrying, derived from the Old English word "descry" meaning "to make out dimly" or "to reveal," is a method of divination that involves gazing into a reflective surface, such as a mirror, water, or a crystal ball. This mystical practice is used to see events from the past, present, or future or to gain insights into the unknown. The term "scrying" is now generally used to refer to divination from almost any medium; however, the most common means are through crystal balls, water, and mirrors.

Scrying has a long history and is present in many cultures worldwide, from the shamanic traditions of the Americas to the seers of Celtic Britain. For the Oracle Witch, scrying offers a unique opportunity to deepen intuition, enhance psychic abilities, and establish a stronger connection with the spiritual realm.

Understanding the Scrying Mediums

Crystal Balls: These are perhaps the most iconic tool for scrying, largely due to their depiction in popular culture. The crystal ball, made of clear, polished quartz or glass, serves as a medium to reflect light and images. Some practitioners claim the ball's spherical shape aids in symbolizing the universe's wholeness, aiding in spiritual communication.

Scrying Mirrors: Scrying mirrors, also known as "magic mirrors," are typically flat pieces of glass painted black on one side. The reflective, dark surface acts as a window to the subconscious mind, facilitating visions and intuitive insights.

Water: Since ancient times, witches, oracles, and seers have used water for scrying. A dark bowl filled with water can serve as an effective scrying tool. The natural properties of water—its fluidity and reflective surface—facilitate psychic visions and symbolize the depths of the subconscious mind.

Scrying Rituals

Before using any scrying tool, it is vital to cleanse and consecrate it. This process purifies the tool, aligns it with your energies, and prepares it for the sacred work of divination.

To cleanse a scrying tool, hold it under running water or leave it outside under a new moon's light. Envision any negative energy being washed away. As you do this, you may wish to say a few words, such as:

"I cleanse this tool of all energies that came before,

May it be pure and clean, ready to explore."

Next, consecrate your tool. This can be done by passing it through the smoke of an incense stick or holding it in the light of a full moon. As you do so, affirm your intention:

"I consecrate this tool in light and love,

Aligned with my will and the stars above."

Opening Your Mind to Visions

To begin scrying, place your chosen tool on a table before you. Dim the lights, light a few candles, and create a peaceful, undisturbed atmosphere. You might also choose to cast a protective circle around you, invoking any deities or spirit guides you work with.

Begin by taking a few deep breaths, grounding and centering yourself. Gaze into your scrying medium, but don't strain your eyes or focus too hard. Let your gaze be soft and relaxed, as if you're looking through the medium, not at it.

As you continue to gaze, you might start to notice a mist or cloud forming in the medium. This is often a sign that the visions are about to begin. Allow your mind to relax further and let the images come to you. They may be abstract symbols, literal scenes, or metaphorical representations. Be open and receptive—don't try to control the process.

Keep a journal nearby to record any images or impressions you receive. They might not make sense immediately, but over time, patterns may emerge, or further meditation may reveal their meaning.

Scrying, like all divination practices, takes practice. It might take several attempts before you start receiving clear images or messages. Remember, the purpose of scrying isn't just about seeing the future—it's a tool for self-discovery, introspection, and spiritual growth.

In the journey of the Oracle Witch, scrying serves as a beacon, shedding light on the paths untaken and the roads ahead. It is more than just an ancient method of seeing; it is a practice that promotes a deeper understanding of one's self and the universe. As you gaze into the depths of your chosen medium, know that you are participating in a sacred tradition that has guided countless souls through the mists of the unknown, into the realms of profound insight and wisdom.

Chapter 14: Tarot Reading for the Oracle Witch

At the heart of every Oracle Witch lies the art of Tarot reading, a core practice that marries intuition, symbolism, and the energies of the universe to provide guidance. Tarot is a mystical tradition dating back centuries, its origins shrouded in mystery, but its power unequivocal. As we delve into the world of Tarot, it's essential to understand that the cards are not deterministic prophecies. Instead, they reflect potentialities based on the energies surrounding us at a given time.

The Tarot Deck and Its Meanings

The standard Tarot deck comprises 78 cards divided into two main groups: the Major Arcana and the Minor Arcana.

The Major Arcana consists of 22 cards representing life's significant events or spiritual lessons. They symbolize universal themes and experiences we all face at different points in our lives. For example, The Fool signifies new beginnings, The Lovers suggest love or partnership, and Death symbolizes transformation or change.

The Minor Arcana consists of 56 cards divided into four suits: Cups, Wands, Swords, and Pentacles. Each suit corresponds to an element – Cups with Water, Wands with Fire, Swords with Air, and Pentacles with Earth. The Minor Arcana reflects everyday situations and challenges. Each suit encompasses an Ace through Ten, along with Court Cards: the Page, Knight, Queen, and King, signifying different stages of life and aspects of personality.

Learning the meanings of each card is a long-term commitment, but don't be daunted. The cards speak through symbols, and symbols evoke the intuition, which is your greatest ally as an Oracle Witch. Start by spending time with each card, immersing yourself in its imagery, and allowing your intuition to inform your understanding.

Tarot Spreads

A Tarot spread is the arrangement of cards drawn in a reading. Different spreads provide various frameworks for understanding the cards. Let's explore a few:

Three-Card Spread: The simplest spread, ideal for beginners or for quick insights. The three cards typically represent past, present, and future. But they can also represent mind, body, spirit, or situation, action, outcome, depending on your question.

Celtic Cross Spread: A more complex, ten-card spread offering a comprehensive view of a situation, its origins, influences, possible outcomes, and the querent's feelings about it.

Horseshoe Spread: A seven-card spread, often used to provide a more detailed view of a situation, exploring past, present, future, and potential obstacles.

Remember, spreads are not rigid. Feel free to adapt or create your own to best suit your needs or the needs of the person for whom you're reading.

Rituals for Tarot Intuition

The power of the Tarot lies not merely in understanding the card meanings and spreads but in harnessing your intuition. Here are a few rituals to help enhance your Tarot intuition:

Cleansing Ritual: Before using your Tarot deck, cleanse it of any residual energy. You can use smoke from sage or palo santo, or place it on a selenite crystal. As you cleanse your deck, imagine any residual energy dissipating, leaving the cards clear and ready to connect with you.

Charging Ritual: Place your deck in the moonlight during the full moon to charge it. As you do this, intend that the deck be infused with the moon's energy, enhancing your intuition during readings.

Connecting Ritual: Spend time connecting with your deck. Sleep with it under your pillow, carry it with you, or meditate with it. Ask the deck to work with you, to communicate clearly, and guide you towards insights.

Shuffling Ritual: As you shuffle your cards before a reading, focus on the question or situation you're seeking guidance about. Imagine your energy and the energy of your question merging with the cards.

Practicing Tarot is an intimate, transformative journey. As you become more attuned to the Tarot's language, you'll find it's a tool not only for divination but for self-reflection and personal growth. Remember, the Oracle Witch's path is ever-unfolding, evolving as we do. Happy Tarot reading!

Chapter 15: Pendulum Divination

The art of pendulum divination, also known as pendulum dowsing, is an ancient practice used by Oracle Witches to gain insight into the unknown. The pendulum serves as a physical manifestation of our subconscious mind, allowing us to access our intuitive and spiritual realms. This chapter will guide you through the process of using a pendulum for divination, including exercises to practice dowsing and rituals to consecrate and connect with your pendulum.

Before diving into the practicalities, let's first understand the concept of pendulum divination. A pendulum is an object, often a small weight on a chain or string, used to detect subtle energy shifts. As an Oracle Witch, you'll use a pendulum to tap into your subconscious and divine energies, seeking answers that lie beyond the conscious mind's grasp.

Choosing a Pendulum

The first step in pendulum divination is selecting a pendulum. This could be as simple as a ring suspended on a piece of string, a crystal suspended on a chain, or a professionally crafted metal pendulum. The key is to choose something that resonates with you, as this personal connection will enhance your divination sessions.

When choosing your pendulum, trust your instincts. Hold different pendulums and see which one feels right. The connection between an Oracle Witch and her pendulum should be strong, and you'll likely feel a pull towards the pendulum that suits you best.

Consecrating Your Pendulum

Once you've chosen your pendulum, the next step is to consecrate it, preparing it energetically for divination. Consecration is a ritual process that cleanses an object of any prior energies and attunes it to your personal energy.

Begin by cleansing your pendulum. This could be done through various methods such as burying it in salt, smudging with sage, or exposing it to moonlight.

After cleansing, hold your pendulum in your hands and close your eyes. Visualize a radiant light streaming from your heart, down your arms, and into the pendulum. Envision this light purifying the pendulum and aligning it with your energy. Recite an affirmation such as, "With light and love, I consecrate this pendulum for divination. May it guide me to truth and clarity."

Connecting with Your Pendulum

Developing a connection with your pendulum is a crucial part of successful divination. This is achieved through regular practice and sincere communication.

Hold the chain of the pendulum and let it hang motionless. Ask it to show you a "yes" answer. Observe the motion. It might be a side-to-side swing, a circular rotation, or a front-and-back movement. Repeat the process asking for a "no" answer. Establishing this dialogue will enable clear communication during your divination sessions.

Practicing Pendulum Divination

Once you're familiar with your pendulum's language, you can start practicing pendulum divination. Start by asking simple yes/no questions to which you already know the answer. This helps in developing trust in your pendulum and your ability to interpret its movements.

When you're ready, move on to unknown questions. Frame your question clearly, and be open to the answer. You may also ask your pendulum to guide you in decision-making. However, always remember that the pendulum is a tool. Ultimately, the final decision should be based on a combination of your intuition, wisdom, and common sense.

Using Pendulum for Chakra Reading

An advanced use of the pendulum is in chakra readings. By holding the pendulum over each chakra, you can detect imbalances in your energy. A clear, circular motion indicates a balanced chakra, while erratic or limited movement can indicate an imbalance.

Pendulum divination is a powerful tool in an Oracle Witch's arsenal. By choosing, consecrating, and connecting with your pendulum, you can access deeper levels of intuition and insight. Practice regularly, be patient with yourself, and trust in the process. Remember that pendulum divination is not about predicting the future, but about seeking guidance from your higher self and the divine energies that surround you. Happy dowsing!

Chapter 16: Runes and Ogham - Ancient Scripts for Divination

In the old, silent days before written history had fully formed, the ancient cultures of Northern Europe devised a cryptic language made up of symbols – an alphabet that whispered of worlds beyond our own. The Runic Futhark and the Ogham of the Celtic people held a primal magic within their forms, a divine gift that transcended their usual applications in inscriptions and writings. These systems of archaic alphabets were harnessed as potent tools for divination, and they continue to serve modern Oracle Witches as a conduit to the unseen world.

Runic Divination

The first of these systems is the Runes, often associated with Norse and Germanic cultures. The Elder Futhark, the most ancient and traditionally used, consists of 24 symbols divided into three groups known as aetts. Each rune is a channel, a representation of universal energies and concepts.

The First Aett

The first aett is associated with Freya, the Norse goddess of love and fertility. It includes eight runes: Fehu, Uruz, Thurisaz, Ansuz, Raido, Kenaz, Gebo, and Wunjo. These runes largely deal with matters of prosperity, journeys, knowledge, and harmonious relationships. Fehu, for instance, signifies wealth and abundance, while Raido represents travel and evolution.

The Second Aett

Tied to the god Heimdall, the second aett comprises Hagalaz, Nauthiz, Isa, Jera, Eihwaz, Perthro, Algiz, and Sowilo. This aett carries a theme of transformation, protection, and revelation. Isa signifies stillness and patience, while Sowilo symbolizes victory and the spiritual illumination of the self.

The Third Aett

The third aett is linked to Tyr, the god of justice and sacrifice, and includes Tiwaz, Berkano, Ehwaz, Mannaz, Laguz, Inguz, Dagaz, and Othala. These runes hold energy of balance, progress, and spiritual awakening. For example, Berkano indicates new beginnings, while Dagaz represents breakthrough and awakening.

Casting runes involves asking a question, drawing one or more runes from a bag, and interpreting their meanings in relation to the query and their orientation.

Runic Ritual

A basic runic divination ritual involves creating a quiet, sacred space and grounding yourself. Visualize your question as you reach into your bag of runes. As you draw a rune, meditate on its symbolism, considering its relevance to your question.

Ogham Divination

Ogham, pronounced 'OH-am,' is another ancient script used for divination, mainly attributed to the Celtic Druids. An Ogham alphabet consists of 20 main characters, or feda, and an additional five 'forfeda'. Each character is associated with a tree or plant, reflecting the deep connection between Druidic practices and the natural world.

The First Aicme

The first group or aicme includes Birch, Luis, Fern, Sail, and Nion. They primarily relate to new beginnings, protection, clarity, wisdom, and transition.

The Second Aicme

The second aicme involves Huathe, Duir, Tinne, Coll, and Quert, associated with magic, strength, transformation, balance, and love, respectively.

The Third Aicme

Muin, Gort, nGéadal, Straif, and Ruis make up the third aicme, reflecting themes of communication, harvest, binding, strife, and change.

The Fourth Aicme

The fourth aicme consists of Ailm, Onn, Úr, Eadhadh, and Idho, symbolizing perception, journey, stability, connection, and endings.

Like rune casting, the casting of Ogham staves involves drawing symbols from a bag and interpreting them in response to a question.

Ogham Ritual

In an Ogham casting, you create a sacred space and meditate on your question. As you reach into your bag of Ogham staves, visualize the trees associated with the staves. Consider their qualities and how they might speak to your query.

Both runes and Ogham are robust, time-honored divination systems. Yet, they are not to be approached lightly; they are languages in their own right, and learning to speak them is part of your journey as an Oracle Witch. Respect their ancient roots and the wisdom they carry, and they will illuminate your path, helping you divine the future and embrace the unknown.

Chapter 17: Embracing the Unknown - The Journey Ahead

As an Oracle Witch, you've journeyed far into the realm of divination, unearthing ancient knowledge, nurturing your intuition, and learning to connect deeply with the universe around you. As we approach the end of this guidebook, let us venture into what could be the most important aspect of your practice: Embracing the Unknown.

Uncertainty is woven into the very fabric of life. The wheel of existence spins on an axis of impermanence and mystery. As human beings, we often find ourselves unnerved by the unknown, finding comfort in predictability and control. Yet, it is this very element of uncertainty that breathes life into our journey as an Oracle Witch. It forces us to embrace change, to evolve, to deepen our understanding of the craft, and to fine-tune our bond with the unseen forces that guide our hand and open our third eye.

As you delve deeper into the realm of divination, remember that it is not merely a tool to predict the future. Divination is an art, a language through which we communicate with the universe. It is a mirror that reflects not only our destiny but also our present, our choices, our fears, and our dreams. It guides us, not through rigid answers, but through signposts and symbols that encourage introspection and personal growth.

You might sometimes be confronted with readings that are difficult to decipher or interpret. This can be frustrating, particularly when you feel the urgent need for clarity. In such moments, take a step back. Breathe. Ground yourself. Remember that every Oracle Witch, from the most novice to the most adept, experiences this. An unclear reading is not a sign of failure, but an invitation to delve deeper, to question more, to reassess your current perspective.

Ask yourself, "What am I missing? What else is there to understand? Is there another way to approach this situation?" These questions will not only help you decipher your reading but also push you to expand your awareness, helping you grow not just as an Oracle Witch, but as a person.

Do not shy away from seeking help. The community of witches, both online and offline, can be an incredible source of wisdom and support. Sharing your experiences and seeking guidance from others can often shed light on an aspect you hadn't considered. Remember, every witch has a unique perspective, influenced by their own unique journey and experiences.

Most importantly, trust your intuition. Your gut feelings are the whispers of your subconscious, the sum of your knowledge and experiences. Even when the cards, runes, or pendulum are unclear, your intuition can provide guidance. Take the time to hone this skill, to listen to that small voice inside you. It's a muscle that grows stronger with use.

At times, you may come across readings that seem negative or unsettling. Understand that every card, every rune, every swing of the pendulum, bears both light and shadow. They merely reflect potentialities and energies, not fixed outcomes. Our actions, our decisions, shape the reality we experience.

In these moments, do not panic or fear. Instead, look at these readings as warnings or advice. They provide an opportunity for introspection and change. They prompt you to ask, "What can I learn from this? How can I transform this energy into something positive?" Always remember, the power to shape your future lies in your hands.

As you progress along the path of the Oracle Witch, never stop learning. This path is not one with a definitive end; it is a lifelong journey of growth and discovery. Read books, attend workshops, learn from mentors, and constantly update your practice. Every day brings new experiences, new wisdom, and new opportunities to deepen your craft.

Embracing the unknown also means accepting that we do not have control over everything. We cannot predict or influence every outcome. This lack of control can be unsettling, but it is a necessary part of our growth. It forces us to trust, to surrender, to accept that some things are beyond our understanding or influence. This acceptance doesn't make us powerless but opens us up to the flow of life, allowing us to ride the waves of change with grace and resilience.

It's crucial to remember that while divination offers profound insights, it does not replace living in the present. Embrace your readings, but also remember to engage fully with the world around you. Experience the magic in everyday life – the silent wisdom of trees, the gentle caress of the wind, the transformative power of the seasons. The future will come in its own time.

Lastly, as you embrace the unknown, remember to also embrace yourself. Cherish your unique journey, your strengths, your vulnerabilities. Celebrate your victories, learn from your mistakes, honor your intuition. You are the Oracle Witch, a divine channel of wisdom, navigating the mysterious dance of fate and free will. Your journey is not just about divining the future; it is about creating it, living it, and cherishing it in all its glorious uncertainty.

Embrace the unknown, for it is there that we find the greatest magic. Trust the journey, trust yourself, and trust the craft. The path of the Oracle Witch is a beautiful, ever-unfolding mystery, ripe with endless potential and infinite possibilities. It is a journey of continual learning, growth, and transformation. So go forth, brave Oracle Witch, and may the wisdom of the universe guide your steps as you dance with the unknown.

Printed in Great Britain
by Amazon